Having a Little Chat with
JESUS

Sr JMdie

Having a Little Chat with
JESUS

An Introduction and Step-by-Step Guide to
Praying to Jesus in the Tabernacle

Sr Josephine Mary Udie

ST PAULS Publishing
ST PAULS by Westminster Cathedral
Morpeth Terrace, Victoria, London SW1P 1EP
Tel: +44 (0) 207 828 5582
www.stpauls.org.uk

ST PAULS Publishing
Moyglare Road, Maynooth,
Co. Kildare, Ireland
Tel: +353 (1) 628 5933
www.stpauls.ie

© 2025 ST PAULS Publishing

Scripture texts are taken from the New Community Bible
Catholic Edition © 2023 St Pauls. Used with permission.

ST PAULS does not necessarily endorse the individual
views contained in its publications.

A catalogue record for this book is available from
the British Library.

ISBN: 978-1-910365-95-3

Printed by Bishops Printers.

ST PAULS is an activity of the priests and brothers
of the Society of St Paul who proclaim the Gospel
through the media of social communication.

Table of Contents

Dedication 07

Foreword 09

How to use this book 13

Why have a 1-2-1 chat with Jesus? 15

What is prayer? 17

How to pray before the Tabernacle 19

Introduction to the parents guide 29

Why introduce children to praying to Jesus in the Tabernacle? 31

The significance of the Tabernacle 33

Explaining prayer to children 35

Praying before the Tabernacle – step by step 37

Conclusion 39

About the author 40

Acknowledgement 41

References 42

Dedication

To all the Children and families of the World.

Foreword

*I*n the many years of my working with children, young people and very often with their families and significant others, there seems to be a common theme that runs through and keeps being raised as a topic for discussion by the children and young people, that is; the eagerness to share with or talk to their friends, their parents or siblings about their experiences or conversations they have had or heard or things they have witnessed. They just can't wait.

However, the time or place may not always be the best or most appropriate to do this. There are also some other times when a child or young person may not want to talk about or share their experience or let out what may be bothering them. Occasionally whilst just walking along, you may find a child sitting quietly, or not participating in the activities going on around them. One of the things I see children or young people struggle with is "the idea of friendship" making or maintaining a close a relationship can be so important for them yet is sometimes difficult to navigate.

A little chat sometimes could prompt an informal conversation when you hear them say things like "she/he does not want to play with me" or "talk to me". At this stage, it may be difficult for them to ask for help from the teacher or even for the teacher to reach out to them immediately to support them. Other times it could be a very critical time when they feel afraid or need someone to listen to them, it could be a desperate situation or needing someone to celebrate with them (at times when they receive an award or a sticker for good behaviour or helping another child with their classwork). Or they may have suffered from bullying.

It was on one such occasion that a child shut a question at me. She suddenly asked me to tell her what I do when I needed to talk to someone or when I was afraid, and how did I handle such situations. Sharing with them some of my own stories or occasions when I have felt the same way led me to better understand their interest and readiness to listen to me and ask me questions about what I did. This made me realise that I needed to share with them the story of my own "secret strategy" i.e. "Having Recourse to My Best Friend" whom I can reach out to at any time, but more so; He is someone, who is always there with me, so much so that I am "NEVER ALONE". Then I added that, this same "friend" is always there for them too. They can invite Him and have a little chat with Him. He is always ready and waiting for us. As Catholics we believe that when we pray before Jesus in the Blessed Sacrament (Jesus in the Tabernacle or the Monstrance), the fullness of His life, power, and love are always present. Jesus is here with you right now! Pray to Him in your own words or your own language. Have a little talk with Jesus. As he says to us "Look, I stand at the door and knock. If anyone hears my voice and opens the door, I will come in to him and have supper with him, and he with me" (Rev. 3:20). In other words, he will come in and share with us. From my own experience, praying before the Blessed Sacrament is awesome. You do not have to talk or say anything, just sit down quietly and listen. It is your own quiet and special time with Jesus.

Jesus wants us to ask for what we need: "Do not be anxious about anything, in everything resort to prayer and supplication together with thanksgiving and bring your requests before God. Then the peace of God, which surpasses all understanding will keep your hearts and minds in Christ Jesus" (Phil 4:6-7).

It is important to remind children and young people that if they ever feel unhappy or distressed, that they should always talk to their parents, guardians or teachers to get support and to ensure that they feel safe. Child safety and protection is very important for all children. We must always make sure that we are doing everything possible to protect children from any risk of harm due to the situation in which they live. Finding a good time to start this conversation helps children to feel relaxed and confident.

It is also important to remember that 'child protection' is part of the Safeguarding process, which includes procedures that detail how to respond to concerns about a child identified as experiencing or likely to experience harm.

Whatever we face, our first option should always be to call upon the name of Jesus Christ, for through that name the foundations are shaken and demons' tremble.

Let us pause for a moment and ask ourselves, "what does having a chat mean?" According to the Cambridge dictionary, it is having an informal conversation with someone. Sometimes that person may not be reachable at that time of greatest need, for example when you just feel like sharing some idea or thought very quickly, or asking a quick question.

These were some of the inspirations that led to my initial thoughts about writing this little book "Having a Little Chat with Jesus". The beauty of a chat is that it does not have to be rigid or follow a formula rather it is informal, simple, reciprocal, it could be on a One-to-One (1-2-1), or among a group of friends.

How to Use this Book

*T*his is not a textbook. It is designed to be used by young people as individuals on their own or with support from their families to enjoy this 1-2-1 relationship with Jesus. I hope you enjoy it. I have added a bit of a guide for parents and carers so that they can help the young ones find a way around reading through it and beginning bit by bit develop a closeness to Jesus, and knowing also that they can always have a little chat with Him at any time of the day or night. I am like a link in a chain, a bond of connections, in the bible story, Philip brought Nathanael to Jesus but before he sees Jesus, Jesus sees him (John 1:43-51). Like Philip, any one of us could be the link in the chain and bringing other people to Jesus; this is a great gift and should not go unheeded. Nathanael asked Jesus, how do you know me? Jesus said to Him, before you saw me, I saw you by the fig tree, the Lord sees us, when no one else sees us, in moments of isolation, in our loneliness, even in our times of peace and serenity, He is there, He sees us. You might ask yourself, why is there power in the name of Jesus? What does His name mean? The name Jesus is a Greek male name meaning "Saviour". God is a friend to whom you do not have to express your sentiments by words; He understands and feels every beat of your heart. You can reveal yourself entirely to Him, even more so than to yourself. He understands and fathoms all your needs, your wishes and your feelings, better than you yourself.

Why have a 1-2-1 chat with Jesus?

A relationship with Jesus can be very comforting. Having a 1-2-1 chat with Jesus in the Tabernacle is a great way to deepen this relationship and get to know Jesus. It will help you to experience unity with Jesus and bond with Him, which will give you **strength and comfort** in times when you need it. Having a relationship with Jesus is to have a friend who is **always there for you**, that you can always depend on, **no matter what.**

Why chat with Jesus in the Tabernacle?

To understand why speaking with Jesus in the Tabernacle is special, we first need to understand what the Tabernacle is.

When you go into church, have you ever noticed a round or square box behind the altar, covered in a beautiful cloth? See if you notice it next time you go. This is called the Tabernacle!

For those of us in the Catholic Faith tradition, we believe that inside the Tabernacle is something very important. This is because the Tabernacle holds the Body and Blood of Jesus Christ – called the **Blessed Sacrament**. Although Jesus is present everywhere, among us and in churches, he is present in the Tabernacle in a very special way because of the Blessed Sacrament and we believe His real presence is there.

You may have also noticed that there is a red candle or oil lamp near the Tabernacle. This is the Tabernacle lamp. When it is lit, it means that the Blessed Sacrament is inside the Tabernacle.

So, it can be comforting to pray in front of the Tabernacle because we know that **Jesus is truly present inside it, showing or indicating the real presence of Jesus at this moment in the church or chapel.**

What Is Prayer?

*P*rayer is **"making time for God and having a simple conversation with Him"**.

There are many ways to pray and you can choose how you'd like to go about it. You can pray silently or out loud. You could use a prayer such as the *Our Father or the Hail Mary*, or you could make up your own words. What is important is that in this moment, you are **focusing on your connection with God**.

How to pray before the Tabernacle

Step 1: Entering the Church

When you come inside the church, either genuflect, kneel, or bow your head towards the Tabernacle, and make the sign of the cross on your forehead. Do the same thing when you leave. In doing this, **you are recognising the presence of Jesus** and saying "Hello" to Him.

This gesture could also mean other things, what you want to say to God is up to you. It could also mean "Jesus, I adore you" or "thank you, Jesus, for bringing me to church", for example.

Step 2: Kneeling or sitting before the Tabernacle

We often kneel to pray because it is a way of **using our whole body** to show that we are aware of Jesus' presence, and that we are honouring Him.

Step 3: Focusing on God

Before saying your prayer, **focus on God**. Remember that **He is there with you while you pray**, and listens to everything you'd like to say to Him. Be attentive and calm so that you may hear or feel His response.

Step 4: Your chat with Jesus

When we meet new friends, we want to get to know them better.

How do we do it? We share our stories. **The same thing happens in prayer**.

There are many ways to pray and connect with Jesus. We could have silent conversations with Him, or we could say the Rosary. We could sing hymns, write in a prayer journal or read from a spiritual book. We could even just sit, looking up at the Tabernacle, and think of God's love in the presence of Jesus.

How you connect with God is up to you. There are some examples on the next page of how a conversation with Jesus could go, if you are unsure of where to begin. Having a chat with Jesus can be as simple as having a chat with any of your friends. Talk to Jesus about what you are interested in, what you are worried about. **He wants to know, He wants to help, and He loves you**.

Step 5: Thanking Jesus, saying goodbye, and leaving

When the time is up, thank Jesus for speaking with you. Ask Jesus to stay with you – explain that you want to know Him better and you want Him to be your friend. The Father, Son, and Holy Spirit live on in you as you go about the rest of your day.

You could say a short prayer like: "Dear Jesus come into my heart, come into my life. Lord Jesus, I ask you to come to me, stay with me. I invite you to come into my heart. Come also to my family; my school; my parish; my community; and to the whole world."

Remember to genuflect, kneel, or bow towards the Tabernacle as you leave the church.

Examples of Prayer

Imagine that Jesus is speaking to you – a conversation between you and Him could go like this:

Example 1:

Jesus: What you are up to today? Would you like to sit with me even if it is for a few seconds? Can you tell me what's on your mind?

You: Nothing much Jesus - I popped in only to see if I could speak with you and share some little things on my mind.

Jesus: Go on, let me hear it all. I am really interested, and I am listening.

Example 2:

You: Dear Jesus, come and walk with me today? I feel a bit tired and alone.

Jesus: Please come and sit here with me.

You: I didn't sleep very well last night. Did you know Jesus, I didn't have a very good meal yesterday either and maybe that's why I didn't sleep very well. Can you help me Jesus?

I know you can because you are my friend.

Jesus: Yes, you know I can, tell me all about it.

You: Jesus, my mum wasn't feeling too well today. Can you visit? Can you come with me and make her feel better?

Jesus: Yes, of course, I will come and will lay my hands on your mum. Tell her how much I love her too and everyone in your family.

You: Thank you so much Jesus, I know I can rely on you, you are such a good friend. You are my very special friend, and I love you too. Can I bring my friend next time to see you?

Jesus: Yes, certainly, bring them along and all your other friends. Tell them I am always waiting to see them.

You: Jesus, can I invite you to my house, my room, my heart? Would you like to stay with me always?

Jesus: Of course, I will come!

You: Can I also invite you to my school, my family and my community?

Jesus: Sure, I would love to come, anytime. God bless you and go in peace.

You: Thank you, Jesus.

Some Written Prayers You Could Say in His Presence:

Prayer of Faith:

"My Jesus I believe in you. I believe you are here truly present, and this is why I came: to listen to you; to have a little chat with you (mention whatever you want to talk to Jesus about):

Worry;

Fear;

Grades;

Parent/s;

Carer;

My sister;

My brother; etc.

Jesus, I trust in you, I know you will answer me (stay quiet and invite Jesus to your heart, listen to what He is saying to you)"

Another very important Prayer you could say before the Blessed sacrament is:

O Sacrament Most Holy

O Sacrament Divine

All praise and all thanksgiving

Be every moment Thine (x 3)

Prayer of Thanksgiving:

"My Jesus, thank you for bringing me to your presence. I am happy I came and thank you so much for listening to me and showing me how much you love and care for me and everyone in my home, family, school and community. I am going back much happier and more rested. Thank you, Jesus, for being so kind and friendly. I am happy I have a friend like you. Will you continue to be my friend?"

Parents and Children:

"Lord, fill us with your love help us to sin no more, give us confidence to remain in your love, we want to be happy and you Lord can give us this happiness, no other one can, only you Lord Jesus can give us this wonderful and special gift."

Other Prayers:

Our Father, Hail Mary, Glory be to the Father.

The Our Father:

Our Father, who art in heaven,

hallowed be thy name;

thy kingdom come; thy will be done

on earth as it is in heaven.

Give us this day our daily bread;

and forgive us our trespasses

as we forgive those who trespass against us;

and lead us not into temptation,

but deliver us from evil.

Amen.

The Hail Mary:

Hail, Mary, full of grace, the Lord is with thee.

Blessed art thou among women,

and blessed is the fruit of thy womb, Jesus.

Holy Mary, Mother of God, pray for us sinners,

now and at the hour of our death.

Amen.

The Glory Be:

Glory be to the Father,

and to the Son,

and to the Holy Spirit.

As it was in the beginning, is now,

and ever shall be

world without end.

Amen

Prayer before the Blessed Sacrament:

O Sacrament Most Holy

O Sacrament Divine

All praise and all thanksgiving be every moment Thine (x 3)

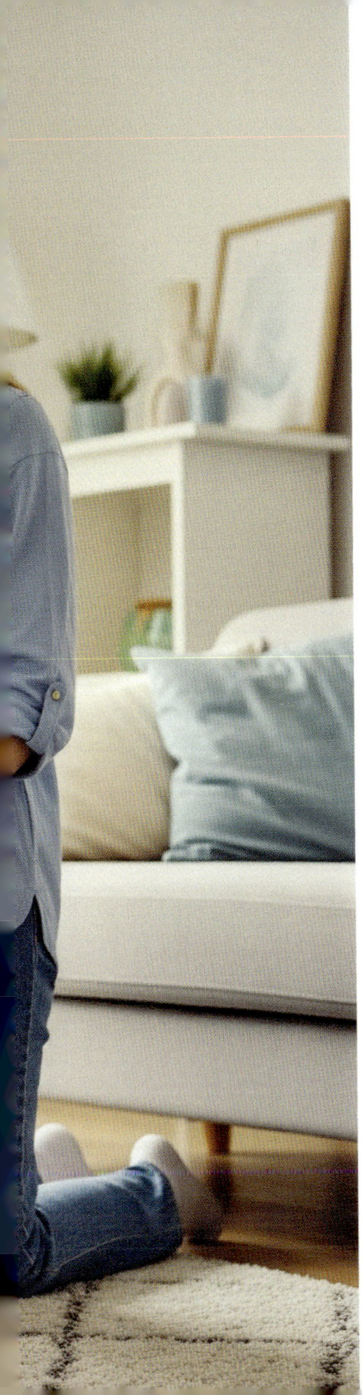

Having a Little Chat with Jesus Guidebook:

Information Guide for Parents and Carers

Introduction to the Parents Guide

The idea of introducing children to prayer can seem like a daunting task. I often get responses such as "Woah, no I don't think so, I can't try it, I'm not sure what to do or how to do it", when talking to parents, or even children and young people themselves, about prayer and praying. To talk about praying in front of the Tabernacle or before the Blessed Sacrament? This could be another 'big ask'… or is it really?

There are many wonderful books out there on praying before the Blessed Sacrament. This little guide is not intended to add to that list. It is, however, a beginner's step-by-step guide for 7-11-year-olds to learn how to pray before Jesus in the Tabernacle. The guide focuses on helping children learn that it is possible to have a 'little chat', prayer or conversation with Jesus in their own quiet time and space and learn that they could refer to Him as their 'friend'. In this way, an attempt is made to teach the child how to grow their relationship with Jesus. When we pray it becomes an opportunity to initiate a relationship with Him in whom we believe and whom we are encouraged to follow in our Christian life. As Pope Francis said: "Our prayer cannot be reduced to an hour on Sundays. It is important to have a daily relationship with the Lord" (Pope Francis @ Pontifex October 2013).

Why introduce children to praying to Jesus in the Tabernacle?

*I*n the Gospel of St. Matthew, Jesus said: "Do not stop the little children from coming to me, for the kingdom of heaven belongs to such as these" (Mt 19:14). Teaching children how to pray in front of the Tabernacle could be one of many ways of bringing children to Jesus. It could help both parents and children realise that this may not be too difficult, and that it may be an effective way of introducing children and young people to building that 1-2-1 relationship with Jesus. It can also teach them how to kneel or sit quietly in front of the Tabernacle, recognising that Jesus is present, that they can now have a 1-2-1 chat with him and share what is on their mind.

Children are naturally filled with wonder about the world and are open to discovering the mystery of God, who gave us our very being and all that we have. This was obvious in a *SteerRight* workshop I was running with a group of 7-11-year-olds. The session was getting too noisy, and as I am used to (probably unconsciously) doing, I made the sign of the cross on my forehead. Suddenly the noise stopped because one of the young people in the group raised his hand and asked me what I was doing and why. I asked if all the children would like to know, they all shouted yes!

I then explained that their noise was so loud, and I was having a quick word with my 'friend up there' to help me. One of the youngest in the group, who was always curious, asked me "did your friend hear you?". I said "yes, He did, and I could see that you were all quiet". "What is your friend's name?" was the next question, and seeing the curiosity on their faces, I went on to explain that His name is Jesus and I always called out to Him when I needed help, whenever I wanted to have a quick 1-2-1 chat with Jesus, share a story with Him or get some reassurance (Matt. 8: 4-13, Mk 9: 17-27). Curiosity grew, and questions continued to be asked about how to reach 'my friend up there', and how we know if He hears us when we speak with Him. Questions like "Can you see Him?", "How do you know He is there?", "How do you know He has answered your prayer?" were asked.

In using their imagination, young children can begin to explore or have a conversation with Jesus. Explaining praying in front of the Tabernacle as a simple conversation with God or having a 1-2-1 chat with Jesus, especially when He is present in the Tabernacle, can lead children to building a beautiful relationship with Jesus.

The importance of listening: becoming aware that Jesus may be saying something to them, and may even ask a simple question or request of them, could be the first step for the children in learning how to listen to Jesus in their close 1-2-1 encounter with Him.

Jesus' request that "Do not stop the little children from coming to me, for the kingdom of heaven belongs to such as these." (Mt 19: 14) shows that Jesus Himself is always waiting for children to come to Him. It is therefore important that we begin early enough to teach children and young people how to pray in front of the Tabernacle. This knowledge that Jesus is truly present in the Tabernacle provides an opportunity for developing and growing in faith, and deepening their relationship with Jesus on a 1-2-1 basis.

The Significance of the Tabernacle

The guide explains the significance and importance of the Tabernacle (see image 2). The following information goes into a little more depth. If you read the guide together with children, you could discuss what is written and answer any questions that come up.

Whether we are visiting church for private, individual prayer or present for Mass, there should be one focal point before our eyes. The place is called the Tabernacle (we see it present in all Catholic churches, as a focal point of prayer). We could draw children's attention to the Tabernacle by talking about the things we see as we enter the church. For example, we could ask them what are the first obvious things they notice? Then describe that the round or square-like box usually covered with a beautiful veil or cloth is the Tabernacle. The red oil lamp or candle burning next to the Tabernacle is the 'Tabernacle lamp'. In most churches, it can be located above the altar or at the side of the altar with the lighted lamp beside it. In some big churches the lamp can be seen hanging from the ceiling above the altar, directly focusing on the Tabernacle where the Blessed Sacrament is kept.

Although Jesus is present among us everywhere and in the churches, he is known to be always present in a very special way within this special place, 'the Tabernacle'. The Tabernacle is a box-like vessel for the exclusive reservation of the consecrated Eucharist. It serves as a secure place in which the Blessed

Sacrament is kept as a focus for meditation and prayers of those who visit the church. After Mass, any consecrated bread which has not been used is placed inside it. Catholics believe that Christ is present in the Blessed Sacrament and therefore it cannot be thrown away, so it is stored in the Tabernacle to be used again and also to bring Holy Communion to the sick who cannot participate in Mass. The sanctuary lamp or Tabernacle lamp signifies that the Blessed Sacrament is present in the Tabernacle.

The lamp is placed by the Tabernacle or hung on a wall of the sanctuary. If it is extinguished, it signifies there is no Blessed Sacrament inside the Tabernacle. Its origins are Exodus 27:20-21: "You are to command the people of Israel to bring you pure olive oil for the lamp, and to keep a flame burning there perpetually. Aaron and his sons are to set this flame in the Tent of Meeting, outside the veil that is before the Testimony. It must burn there before the LORD from evening to morning perpetually. This is an irrevocable statute for all generations of Israelites."

Explaining Prayer to Children

There are many definitions of prayer but for this purpose we shall use this definition: "prayer is making time for God and having a simple conversation with him". Daily prayer is how we respond to God's invitation to a deeper relationship that nurtures our spiritual well-being. As a community of believers, we find great joy in sharing our spiritual blessings. This includes introducing children to the gift of prayer.

We can also define prayer as 'lifting up our hearts and minds to God'. In other words, bringing our focus to this special moment of connection with God. It could be silent or said out loud. It could use a prescribed set of words, or a person's own words. In prayer, Christians lift their minds and hearts to God. There are many kinds of prayers, including:

- adoration - praising God for his greatness and admitting dependence on him
- confession - owning up your sins and asking for God's mercy and forgiveness
- thanksgiving - thanking God for his many blessings, e.g. health or children
- petition - asking God for something, e.g. healing, courage or wisdom
- intercession - asking God to help others who need it, e.g. the sick, poor, those in need

Praying Before the Tabernacle – Step by Step

Step 1: Entering the Church

The first step on entering the church is to encourage them to either genuflect, kneel, or bow their head towards the Tabernacle as they enter and leave the church, and make the sign of the cross on their forehead. By making the sign of the cross and saying a short prayer, we show that we recognize the presence of Jesus and say "hello" to Him, "Jesus, I adore you", or "thank you Jesus for bringing me to the church".

It is important for children to know why we kneel. "We kneel because Jesus is here in a special way." For us Catholics, the purpose of kneeling is to allow the worshipper to engage his whole person in acknowledging the presence of and to honour Jesus Christ in the Holy Eucharist. It is customary to genuflect whenever one comes into or leaves the presence of the Blessed Sacrament reserved in the Tabernacle.

Step 2: Kneeling or sitting before the Tabernacle

Kneel or sit down quietly before Jesus in the Tabernacle. Encourage children to try to be faithful to spending at least 5 to 10 minutes daily alone with God. Try to make room for this at a regular time each day. God wants time to be alone with each of us and to communicate with us; and what God wants from us, God deserves. Encourage children to be happy to listen quietly and openly, as if they are sitting in their parent's lap, listening to a story.

Step 3: Focusing on God

Encourage children to focus on God before saying their prayer. Remind them that God is there with them while they pray, and that God is listening to every word that is being prayed. Be attentive and receptive to God's voice during the prayer. Individuals must first seek to be filled with the Spirit of God if they desire to lead a deeper, more spiritual and more fulfilled life.

Step 4: Their chat with Jesus

Teaching children to appreciate spending quiet time in the presence of the Tabernacle (even as part of their preparation for first holy communion) and introducing them to the Tabernacle helps them understand why this is the main focus in the church – because it houses Jesus.

Guide the children in prayer, pausing to allow the children to pray quietly. You could give instruction such as: "In your prayer, tell God about your favourite foods. God wants to hear what you like best. If you like, thank God for giving you food to eat today."

Step 5: Thanking Jesus, saying goodbye and leaving

When the time is up, encourage children to thank God for speaking to them. They could invite Jesus to come into their hearts, to enrich their lives. Remind them that Father, Son and Spirit live on in them as they move away to continue the rest of their day.

This prayer is in the guide to facilitate this: "Dear Jesus come into my heart, come into my life. Lord Jesus, I ask you to come to me, stay with me. I invite you to come into my heart. Come also to my family; my school; my parish; my community; and to the whole world."

Conclusion

As Jesus travelled on his journeys, he often paused to pray to his heavenly Father. Jesus's own disciples were inspired by watching Him pray and asked Jesus to teach them how to pray. When children see us pray, they, like Jesus's disciples, are also inspired to know how to grow closer to God in prayer. Each one of us is called to hand on the gift of faith to children and to teach them the different forms and expressions of prayer – including spontaneous prayer, liturgical prayer, and reflective prayer – that will empower them to build a lifelong dialogue and relationship with Jesus.

About the Author

A Life Dedicated to Service

Reverend Sister Josephine Udie's journey as a Member of a Catholic Religious Institute of Nuns and Lay People called Missionary Community of the Holy Spirit (MCHS) has taken her across the globe, where she has ministered to countless young people and families. Her experiences have instilled in her a profound understanding of human dignity, recognising each individual as a beloved child of God.

Driven by her passion for empowering others, Sister pursued training as a Power Coach and Healthcare Professional. She leverages her skills and channels her passion to support and inspire children and families to reach their full potential.

As the Director and Project Coordinator of *SR Life-Style Coaching (SteerRight), Sister embodies the organisation's motto: "Little Help, Big Difference" by highlighting the effectiveness of how a small intervention can have a powerful impact. Her dedication to making a positive impact is evident in her various roles, including her academic achievements and professional certifications. She has spent many years working in UK, in the Educational, Community Health & Social Care Sectors including Schools, Colleges and the National health Service NHS.

A devout Catholic, Sister's faith has been the cornerstone of her life. She has led numerous liturgical celebrations and continues to inspire others through her unwavering commitment to Jesus Christ. Her ability to embrace challenges with a positive attitude and a steadfast belief in God's plan is a testament to her strong faith and resilience.

Jesus said, "See that you do not despise any of these little ones" (Mt 18:10).

**SR Life-Style Coaching website: www.steerright.org.uk*

Acknowledgement

I offer my heartfelt thanks to Almighty God for the grace and strength to undertake this work. I am eternally grateful to the Blessed Virgin Mary, Our Mother, whose intercession has guided and inspired me. May the Lord Jesus Christ, Our Savior, be glorified through these pages.

I am indebted to my twin brother Fr. Andor Thomas Udie, whose unwavering support has been a constant source of encouragement. I also express my sincere gratitude to Diana Wilson, Maureen Evans, Clare Herriot and Kimie Cherrie Rees, MJ, the young people at St George Primary School, Bickley, London, and St Vincent's Catholic Primary School, Bromley, London and St Pauls Publishing, UK for their invaluable assistance in editing and providing insightful suggestions. There are so many others for whom I would like to offer my thanks but cannot mention all their names. They are all in my prayers.

Finally, I wish to acknowledge the contributions of the young people whose creativity and enthusiasm have enriched this project. May their participation in this work deepen their relationship with the Lord.

Sources referenced

1. The New Community Bible, 2008.
2. What every child should know about Prayer, Nancy Guthrie, 2018.
3. The Jesus Story Book Bible Anglicised Edition, Sally Lloyd-Jones, Jago, 2012.
4. Influencing Children to become World Changers, Joy Dawson, 2003.
5. The Catholic Children's Prayer Book, Louis M. Savary, 1985, 2003, 2007.
6. Anything you ask, Colin Urquhart, 1979.
7. Jesus Our Redeemer: A Christian Approach to Salvation, Gerald O'Collins. SJ 2007.
8. Images used are AI generated.